Original title:

Sprouts of Solitude

Copyright © 2025 Creative Arts Management OÜ
All rights reserved.

Author: Beckett Sinclair
ISBN HARDBACK: 978-1-80581-778-9
ISBN PAPERBACK: 978-1-80581-305-7
ISBN EBOOK: 978-1-80581-778-9

The Softness of Solitude

In a garden of whispers, I sit alone,
With weeds my only friends, they've brightly grown.
I chat with a gnome who's lost his hat,
He laughs and says, 'Well, how about that!'

My tea is lukewarm, brewed by thin air,
A squirrel steals cookies, if I only dare.
I hold a debate with a stubborn chair,
In this company, I find life quite rare.

Clouds float like giants, I wave and they wave,
Each puff floating by, my heart they do save.
Conversations with pillows, they never stray,
But sometimes they whisper, 'You've slept half the day!'

The sun plays a trick, it tickles my nose,
While shadows perform in a dance, oh so close.
A ballet of dust will surely appear,
In the silence, I chuckle, no one can hear.

Rustling Leaves of Lonesomeness

In the park, I'm all alone,
My thoughts, like leaves, have overgrown.
An acorn fell and gave a grin,
Said, "Hey buddy, join my spin!"

The bench knows all my rhymes and jests,
It holds my laughs, it holds my quests.
A squirrel mocked my absent friends,
Leaving me laughing 'til daylight ends.

The Alchemy of Quiet Moments

In silence, I stir my tea in dreams,
The kettle whistles, and all it seems.
A flick of dust, a tiny dance,
Turns solitude into a jolly chance.

I talk to chairs, they're great at loaning,
They listen well, their comfort's moaning.
A spider spins some jokes on me,
Says, "You're the best, just wait and see!"

Seeds of Serenity

I planted hopes in a tiny pot,
Watered with giggles, but not a lot.
They sprouted up with little sighs,
Surprised at clouds and sunny skies.

A gnome nearby just rolled his eyes,
At my attempts to flower wise.
But in the soil, a burp did bloom,
And laughter echoed through my room.

One Among Many

In a crowd, I'm mostly air,
Floating 'round without a care.
A mime waves hi, I strike a pose,
Not quite sure how this one goes.

A single donut rolls my way,
With sprinkles bright, it joined the fray.
Together we laughed at all the throng,
Finding joy, where I belong.

The Quiet Symphony of Nature

In the forest, whispers play,
A squirrel giggles, chasing gray.
Trees dance slowly with a grin,
While crickets practice for a win.

A bear snores loud, a comical feat,
As birds crack jokes, can't be beat.
Rabbits hop with silly flair,
Nature's theater, laughter in the air.

The Hidden Oasis Within

In a small pond, frogs perform,
With silly leaps, they break the norm.
Dragonflies wear tiny hats,
Chasing each other, imagine that!

Willows sway and flutter about,
While fish debate on who's the stout.
Bubbles rise with giggles and twirls,
In this oasis, joy unfurls.

Lonesome Landscapes

Mountains high with snowy crowns,
Whisper secrets, giggles abound.
Clouds drift lazily, tickled pink,
Even the rocks chuckle, I think.

Deserts hide a cactus grin,
While lizards dance and spin to win.
A tumbleweed rolls by in style,
Making even the sun crack a smile.

Between Shadows and Light

In the twilight, shadows leap,
Playing games, a secret keep.
The moon winks, a playful sight,
While stars giggle with delight.

A lamp posts jostle, fence in hand,
As shadows form a playful band.
Laughter spills between the trees,
In this light, nothing's as it seems.

The Solace of Stillness

In a quiet nook, I sit and freeze,
My cat's judgment sharp, I've lost my keys.
Fish in a bowl, they laugh at my plight,
But I'm just here, enjoying the light.

The plants gossip, whispering tales,
About my snacks and their failed sales.
A couch potato with chips as my friends,
In this calm chaos, the awkward never ends.

Branches of Reflection

Underneath the tree, I ponder my fate,
A squirrel approaches, eyeing my plate.
I offer a chip, he cocks a sly grin,
Turns out, he has better guests than kin.

The branches sway, they tease my hair,
Shadows play tag, I'll never compare.
With every rustle, they scribble a note,
Oh to be a leaf, just drifting afloat.

The Color of Silence

In a room so quiet, I snack on a treat,
The crunch of the chip is my heartbeat's beat.
Silent as ninjas, my crumbs take flight,
They tumble and dance in the dim candlelight.

Each look from the fridge brings a light-hearted jest,
The cheese winks back, it's clearly the best.
And in this hush, a giggle will creep,
As the leftovers plot, while I take a leap.

Lanterns in the Dark

With lanterns lit, I navigate fate,
Stumbling on shadows, I contemplate.
I trip on a book, it falls with a thud,
A laugh joins the night, echoing with bud.

Oh, the candles wink like playful sprites,
Flickering dreams and fantastical sights.
In this lively gloom, the echoes all chime,
Who knew solitude could be so sublime?

Solitary Growth

In a tiny pot, I sit with glee,
My plant seems to enjoy this spree.
Alone, we argue over soil depth,
While I sip my tea, feeling quite adept.

It wiggles roots like a dance so sly,
While I just stare with a balmy sigh.
Together we thrive, just me and it,
A duo like no other, isn't that a hit?

Unfurling in the Dark

In the night, I hear a creak,
My lonely leaf, so bold and sleek.
It stretches wide, a little alarmed,
Saying, "Hey, I'm quite charmed!"

I chuckle low, as it flutters about,
While wondering what plants chat about.
"I'm the best," it sways in pride,
As I nod along, my sleep denied.

A Garden of One

In my backyard, a flower does bloom,
Declaring the garden's one-man room.
"Look at me," it shouts with delight,
While I roll my eyes at this singular sight.

Its petals wave, like hands in the breeze,
As I giggle, shivering with unease.
I snap a picture for social acclaim,
"World's loneliest bloom," it'll be my claim!

The Resilience of Remoteness

Here I stand, my cactus on display,
All spiky and proud, steering chaos away.
"From the crowd, I thrive," it spins with cheer,
While I ponder if it's lonely here.

With no company, it stands quite tall,
Claiming, "Being alone is fun, after all!"
I laugh aloud, "Oh, little green friend,
In solitude's charm, do we both transcend?"

Lush Loneliness.

In my garden, weeds dance with glee,
They invited a snail, but he's too sleepy.
A bird joined in, singing offbeat,
Where's the rhythm? Oh, what a treat!

Plants gossip quietly, it's a sight,
Chit-chatting grasshoppers deep in the night.
The sunflower, with its big, yellow grin,
Says, "I'm the star, let the show begin!"

Whispers in the Quiet

Silence tiptoes, it's playing peek-a-boo,
While the moon guffaws, feeling quite blue.
A lonely leaf falls, doing a twirl,
Says, "Look at me, I'm a lonely whirl!"

A pebble chuckles, it's seen it all,
From ants in a parade to a leaf's downfall.
In this hush, the shadows play chess,
And the breeze takes bets, what a weird mess!

The Garden of One

One flower sways, with no pals around,
Chatting with bugs, it's a one-sided sound.
The sun laughs, says, "What a bouquet!"
But the flower just sighs, wishing for a fray.

A lone gnome chuckles, it's a dull day,
Sipping on dew, in his own funny way.
"I'm the king here! My kingdom's so small,
But in my heart, I rule over all!"

Echoes of the Seed

A single seed, quite the dramatic act,
Rolling around, trying to make an impact.
It murmurs to soil, "Hey, don't be shy,
Let's grow a tall tale, just you and I!"

The wind joins in, with a giggle so light,
Sways the seedling, oh what a sight!
"I'm not alone, I've got my dreams,
And a wobbly dance, or so it seems!"

Kinship with Shadows

In corners dark, they dance with glee,
Making faces just for me.
Their whispers tickle my silly bones,
Together we share our quirks and tones.

They stretch and yawn, we laugh aloud,
A family formed from shadows proud.
Playing tag on the wall's embrace,
In my mind, they give a warm chase.

They wear their shapes with such finesse,
Creating chaos, I must confess.
With every flicker, they make me grin,
My shadow friends, my loyal kin!

As daylight fades, we play our part,
Oh, to be a shadow, a quirky art.
In the silence, we sing our song,
In this room where we all belong.

Isolation's Gentle Charms

Alone but never truly bare,
I've got my thoughts to keep me fair.
A cup of tea and comfy socks,
Chatting with the lonely clocks.

They tick away with such delight,
Telling stories late at night.
With every chime, a giggle flows,
At all the secrets no one knows.

The couch becomes my trusted friend,
We share our laughs, no need to pretend.
Binge-watching my thoughts on repeat,
Who needs others when I've got this seat?

In my bubble, I find the fun,
Making mischief with everyone.
So here's to peace and playful cheer,
In the quiet, my heart feels clear.

The Beauty of Aloneness

A single flower blooms so bright,
It waves at clouds, a lovely sight.
With petals soft, it sways in style,
Sipping sunshine with a smile.

The mirror mocks my dance today,
Cracking jokes in a funny way.
Who knew my moves could make me laugh?
In this solo act, I'm the autographic craft!

I twirl through puddles, splash and play,
On my own, I'm a cabaret!
With every wink the world will see,
The beauty found in just being me.

So here I stand, a one-man show,
In a crowd of thoughts, I'm never low.
Aloneness, dear friend, is a giggle shared,
In the journey of life, I'm unprepared.

A Secret Language of Leaves

The rustling branches start to speak,
With giggles hidden, secrets peak.
They whisper tales of days gone by,
As breezes weave their lullaby.

In every crack, a chuckle lives,
As nature shares what laughter gives.
A dance of twigs with swaying grace,
In this chatty grove, I find my space.

They tickle the air with cheeky chime,
A card of jokes—oh, I bide my time.
With every rustle, a punchline swings,
The best of humor that nature brings.

So let them converse, with me in tow,
In the secret tongue that leaves bestow.
With giggles twirling in the sun's soft glow,
I join the trees, in this funny show.

The Stillness That Breathes

In quiet corners, laughter lies,
A dance of shadows where silence flies.
My cat's my only, fur-ball mate,
We share our secrets, both learning late.

The toaster hums a soft refrain,
While my thoughts wander, free as rain.
A sock's gone rogue, it's lost its pair,
In this stillness, it's everywhere!

The plants are gossiping, or so I think,
Their leaves whispering over lemonade pink.
Strange companions in the mist of night,
Together we giggle, embracing the light.

Yet here I sit, with a cheese puff snack,
Contemplating why I can't sit back.
A one-person party, balloons in my head,
'Just blame it on cat,' the toast nearly said.

Shadows of a Lonely Heart

Beneath the stars, my shadow sways,
A dance of mischief in lonely bays.
I trip on thoughts like rocks of glee,
And laugh at echoes, all there might be.

The fridge hums a symphony at dawn,
An orchestra of pickles, this is my con.
The lonely cucumber, forlorn and blue,
Makes plans with the mustard, too good to be true.

I stroll through gardens of tangled weeds,
Admiring the loneliness that softly breeds.
A sunflower winks, "Let's have some fun!"
While bees swipe glances, all on the run.

As shadows grow longer, I start to cheer,
Every breeze a tickle, every laugh sincere.
I spy a ladybug dressed for a ball,
In the company of ants, they'll have a brawl!

Petals in the Wind

Whispers of petals, oh what a treat,
Dancing around like they're on their feet.
A rogue leaf flirts, then trips on a stem,
That wind just giggled, what a funny gem!

In fields of daisies, I trip and spin,
Catching the sun on my freckled chin.
Every twist and turn brings a quirky cheer,
As I stomp on the daisies, "I'm sorry, dear!"

A butterfly hiccups, mid-flutter and sway,
Laughter erupts in a whimsical play.
They tease each other, "Hey, look at me!"
While pollen-coated bees buzz in glee.

With each gust of air, tales start to bloom,
My solitude giggles, we share a room.
Nature's a clown, wearing sunshine instead,
Come join the dance in this garden of dread!

Solitude's Embrace

A cozy nook with a blankie wrap,
My thoughts tumble out like a wild trap.
The couch, my throne, where I reign supreme,
With snacks as my subjects, oh what a dream!

The odd sock whispers of journeys past,
Adventures it had while I slept fast.
And the chair with the squeak has stories to tell,
Of all the times it held me so well.

I chat with the coffee mug full of cheer,
It replies in sips, so crystal clear.
"I once was on a table at a grand feast,
Now here I stay, in solitude's beast."

Yet every moment, with tea in hand,
I giggle at life, its funny command.
For in this embrace, I find my way,
Amongst giggling shadows, where I long to stay.

Whispers of Quiet Corners

In corners dark, a cat does stare,
A sock's lost mate, can it still care?
A tumbleweed rolls by with grace,
While I debate my underwear's place.

Mice run races, unseen, unheard,
In my chipped cup, they draft a word.
A sandwich waits for its big break,
But who will take it? Not this cake!

Chairs convene in silence grim,
Sharing tales of bugs and whim.
A plate of cheese, it's feeling blue,
With crackers crumbling, oh, who knew?

So here I sit, an audience grand,
To this odd circus that life has planned.
With tea gone cold and thoughts gone wild,
I laugh alone, a whimsical child.

Seeds of Stillness

In a world where quiet pests reside,
A gnome awaits on the windowside.
He stares at me with painted eyes,
And I wonder if he tells me lies.

My plants don't chatter, they just grow,
But I swear I heard them say hello.
A spider weaves a web of dreams,
While I plot schemes with crazy themes.

An empty chair plays peek-a-boo,
With ghosts of friends who never grew.
The fridge hums tunes of late-night snacks,
While my willpower sadly cracks.

The dust bunnies form a band so slick,
Aware that I'm too slow, too thick.
And in this hush, I find delight,
In giggles shared with shade and light.

Echoes in a Silent Garden

In my garden there's a curious tree,
That whispers secrets just to me.
A worm declares, 'I'm quite a star!'
While daisies roll their eyes from afar.

The lawn gnomes share their spicy tales,
Of long-lost dreams and paper sails.
A toad croaks lore of ancient knights,
While bees buzz off on daring flights.

With every breeze, a giggle comes,
As squirrels perform acrobatics, drums.
A cabbage dreams of a grand parade,
While I stand here, my plans delayed.

Nature's humor, oh so sly,
Gives bedtime stories to the shy.
In the blooms and chatter that feels so grand,
I find joy in this whimsical land.

The Bloom of Isolation

Inside my room, the dust bunnies prance,
Dressed in wisdom, they teach me to dance.
A pillow whispers jokes by the light,
While shadows giggle, tucked in tight.

The old fridge hums a classic tune,
As I debate if it's lunch or a croon.
The laundry piles up with curious charms,
Each sock winks at me, spreading alarms.

A lamp flickers like it's shy,
While I tell it tales of cloudless sky.
The chair sighs deep from standing still,
In this quiet jest, it gets a thrill.

So here I remain, with laughter and time,
In this goofy solitude, I dare to rhyme.
With every echo that fills these walls,
I find the joy in my little stalls.

The Solitude's Embrace

In a chair that squeaks with glee,
I talk to my plants, they laugh at me.
My cat rolls eyes, disdainful of chat,
While I share tales of the fridge and the mat.

The bread's gone stale, the milk is a ghost,
But who needs a party? I'm my own host!
I wear mismatched socks, a crown of old tinsel,
In my cozy kingdom, where silence is a pencil.

Fragrant Dreams in Quiet Places

In the kitchen, I ponder, a spoon in my hand,
Dance with cabbages, they understand.
A whiff of laundry lingers around,
I've lost my socks, but hey, I've found sound!

The herbs in the pot have secretive chats,
They gossip of sunshine and sneaky old bats.
With every stir, I concoct some delight,
I'm a chef of the lone, in the still of the night.

Beneath the Silent Skies

The stars roll their eyes as I sing out of tune,
My garden and I dance under the moon.
A rogue snail treats me like his top fan,
While crickets applaud, they're part of the plan.

The breeze whispers secrets, a giggle or two,
I wave at the shadows, they wave back, it's true!
Moths flutter by in their fantastic disguise,
We throw a bash, no one else comes by.

Uncharted Wilderness Within

In the depths of my mind, I explore with a grin,
Chasing wild daydreams, let the adventures begin!
Pajama-clad hunters, questing for treats,
Find treasure in cookies and unending repeats.

A safari of thoughts, they wander and roam,
Mapping out snacks, as I sit in my dome.
The wilderness laughs, a one-person show,
While I navigate nonsense, in my cozy whoa.

Unlikely Refuge

In a nook where the socks do dwell,
A lonely shoe sings quite a swell.
With mismatched laces and tales to tell,
It dreams of dances, oh so well.

A sandwich waits, half-eaten, forlorn,
Its crusty side is rugged and worn.
In this corner, a party is born,
With crumbs of joy, no one can scorn.

A cactus brags of its prickly charms,
While houseplants offer their leafy arms.
With dust bunnies lining their farms,
They plot together until the alarm.

A lonely cat, a ticking clock,
Share secrets in their quiet block.
While socks barter tales of a sockshock,
In this odd kinship, they unlock.

Hushed Revelations

Behind the curtain, shadows sway,
A lost remotes begins to play.
Each flicker, each buzz leads the way,
To whispered truths of the laundry bay.

The coffee mug, half full, confides,
In sips and drips, its warmth abides.
With sugar cubes that roll and glide,
It keeps the secrets that time hides.

In a closet, far out of sight,
Old board games stir in the night.
"Let's play Monopoly!" they delight,
Even if they only ever fight.

A mirror glimmers with witty glances,
As socks have secret spicy dances.
Their whispers echo, fate enhances,
In a solo space, they take their chances.

Nature's Hidden Refuge

Amidst the weeds, a snail gives chase,
To dandelions in a sweet race.
Disguised as a flower, it finds its place,
In a world of green, no need for grace.

A frog croaks jokes from his lily pad,
While a squirrel reflects, feeling a tad.
With every leap, new laughs are had,
In this nature's giggle, oh-so-rad.

The wind teases trees, a nature's tease,
Tickling leaves like a playful breeze.
In this serene and leafy sneeze,
Birds chart their routes, ~just like keys~.

A raccoon rummages through a bin,
His findings spark a raucous grin.
In this hidden world, where fun begins,
Even trash can host a wild kin!

A Sanctuary of Solace

In a jam jar, fireflies convene,
They share their thoughts, a twinkling scene.
With each tiny flicker, they feel serene,
Dreaming of nights where glowworms preen.

A rubber duck floats on a whim,
In bubbly waters, it learns to swim.
With a quack and wiggle, it won't grow dim,
In this curious calm, on a joyful brim.

A sock puppet waves with a cheerful grin,
Performing plays where sillies win.
With buttons for eyes, it pulls you in,
In a realm of laughter free from sin.

Pixie dust floats, but takes its time,
As fairies dance in sync, sublime.
In this quiet place, they spin and climb,
Creating charades that feel like rhyme.

A Dance of Shadows and Light

In the garden where daisies speak,
A cat trips on mice, oh so sleek.
While sunbeams waltz with shadows bold,
A butterfly's joke never gets old.

The gnomes giggle in silent cheer,
As night creeps in with a raucous leer.
The moon throws a party in the sky,
While crickets compose a lullaby.

Weeds wear hats made from cloud fluff,
Their dance partners? Just a bit tough.
Oh, what a riot in nature's hall,
Where even the tired wish to sprawl!

Yet amongst the chaos, laughter grows,
In a world where whimsy overflows.
And so we twirl with funny delight,
In this grand dance of shadows and light.

Nature's Private Confession

The trees whisper tales to the wind,
Of squirrels that forget where they've been.
A rusty old bench sighs with glee,
While flowers gossip about Bumblebee.

A snail tells tales of his slow, slow trip,
While snickering leaves join in the quip.
The grasshoppers leap in laughter and play,
At the clumsiness of the ants in their sway.

The river bubbles with secrets galore,
As fish swim by, with laughter at their core.
Each pebble chuckles in the sun's warm glow,
In a paradise where giggles freely flow.

So come join the chorus, feel the breeze,
Nature's spa where even the bushes sneeze.
In this woodland of whimsy, don't be shy,
Every tree has a tale, oh me, oh my!

The Thread of Togetherness in Aloneness

Tangled threads in a fabric of space,
A gusty wind gives them a chase.
While lonely socks moan in the drawer,
Searching for partners they can adore.

A wolf howls at the full moon's face,
But even he can't deny the grace.
Of fireflies gathering for a ball,
Twinkling together, one and all.

The coffee pot whistles a solo tune,
While paper cups dream of a picnic in June.
A cactus blinks, on a shelf all alone,
Hoping for company, just a phone.

In aloneness, we find our glee,
A solitary dance, just you and me.
In the threads of our hearts, we always blend,
Where even the loners are never without friends.

The Muffled Symphony of Growth

In a corner where daisies bloom,
A worm hums softly, lost in gloom.
But rain taps gently, a rhythmic cheer,
As plants sway slowly, with nothing to fear.

A tree stretches high, in a dance of grace,
While squirrels perform their nutty race.
The soil giggles as roots intertwine,
In this muffled symphony, all is divine.

Bunnies hop by, with nary a care,
Trying their best to not spill the affair.
Each leaf holds whispers of silly dreams,
As nature chuckles in soft flowing streams.

So let's sway with the rhythm of earth,
In every giggle lies a rebirth.
For in the quiet, growth sings so sweet,
A hilarious dance, where life and laughter meet.

Under the Gaze of the Stars

Beneath the twinkle of each star,
I wonder what's bizarre and far.
Do aliens sip tea on Mars?
Or do they just drive fancy cars?

Moonlight whispers jokes so bright,
While shadows dance in sheer delight.
Do crickets laugh when we can't see?
What secrets lie in that old tree?

The Journey Within

I tried to explore my own back yard,
But tripped on a rake—it hit me hard.
A quest for wisdom, with each small bruise,
Turns out my thoughts were just a snooze.

The fridge calls out with tasty treats,
In solitude, delicious feats.
Lost in dreams of pizza and pie,
Perhaps to journey, I'll just lie?

Solitary Notes on a Breeze

A tune floats by on a gentle air,
Is it a song, or my wild hair?
They say it's quiet, this life so sweet,
But I'll hum along with two left feet.

A wanderer's whimsy upon a breeze,
Twirling around like a pair of keys.
Do rock stars sit alone and fret?
Or is it just a guitar pet?

Echoes of a Peaceful Heart

In the stillness, my heart does play,
Each beat a joke, a funny ballet.
My laughter echoes, light as a feather,
Finding joy in stormy weather.

A tranquil pond reflects my face,
Is it a smile or a funny grace?
Riding waves of silence rare,
I'll chuckle softly, and not a care.

The Silent Growth of Hope

In the corner, a plant sings,
Whispers of joy on little wings.
Leaves dance to a silent tune,
Waiting for a lazy moon.

A pot of soil, a secret friend,
Conversations that never end.
Imaginary tea they brew,
While I pretend I'm not in view.

Roots tickle through the earth below,
"Just a little more, and I will grow!"
They never seem to tire or yawn,
While I just binge-watch till dawn.

In my mind, they plot and scheme,
Running races in a dream.
Oh to join that leafy race,
But here I am, stuck in place.

Dwelling in Quietude

In my room, a pen speaks loud,
Scribbles thoughts, under a cloud.
A quiet mouse takes up the pen,
Writing tales of cats and men.

Dust bunnies gather for a show,
Waltzing in the sun's warm glow.
Each tumbleweed of fluff does dance,
While I sit here, lost in trance.

"Is that a book or a pizza slice?"
Tipping over, just like my dice.
Pages flutter, but the mouse stays,
While I ponder my laundry ways.

A sock declares, "I've got your back!"
While missing its partner, all out of whack.
In quietude, this place is fun,
Where solitude's a party for one.

A Voyage Through Still Waters

A lonely boat drifts on a pond,
It sings a song, quite fond.
The oars just giggle, don't make a fuss,
While turtles laugh, taking the bus.

A fish jumps out, does a splashy jig,
Winks at a frog, who's rather big.
"Hey there buddy, let's ride the breeze!"
But the frog just snores with ease.

Clouds above trade stories in white,
They share jokes about the night.
While the boat takes a nap in the sun,
It dreams of adventures, just for fun.

"Here we float, without a care!"
Says the breeze, tousling my hair.
In stillness, joy has found its place,
As laughter ripples through this space.

The Unseen Blossoming

In a jar, a seed takes a peek,
"Hello world!" it gives a squeak.
Wiggling roots like a little worm,
"This quiet life has such a charm!"

Sunbeams tickle, making it grin,
"I'm growing here, just wait, begin!"
While shadows plot a mischievous scheme,
A tulip yawns, chasing a dream.

Bugs hold tiny, invisible shows,
Debating where the flower goes.
"Let's race to the potting bench, hurry!"
While I just sit, feeling a flurry.

Pollen dust floats like a fine icing,
Making all plans rather enticing.
In the garden of glee, where whispers bloom,
Even solitude has a sense of room.

Roots in the Void

In a garden where no one goes,
The weeds have formed a quiet pose.
They gossip 'neath the daytime sun,
While dandelions laugh at everyone.

The carrots play a hide-and-seek,
With radishes both round and sleek.
The potatoes tell old jokes quite bold,
And mock the flowers, so young, so old.

But one sprout waved and said hello,
To passing clouds and busy crow.
The garden chuckled, feeling bright,
In solitude, they found delight.

Though no one visits this green retreat,
The vegetables have a lively beat.
In the silence they thrive and dance,
Two peas in a pod in a subtle romance.

Blossoms of the Unseen

In hidden nooks where no one dares,
A bunch of mushrooms plays in pairs.
They tickle roots and giggle soft,
As squirrels above them leap aloft.

The wildflowers send notes so sweet,
To blades of grass, a secret treat.
Each petal winks and shares a grin,
Spinning tales of the breeze within.

A solitary bee hums a tune,
While shadows dance beneath the moon.
They throw a party for the night,
With glittering stars as their big light.

In this quiet, wondrous place,
Where plants wear smiles upon their face,
They celebrate their leafy fate,
In laughter loud, they cultivate.

Petals on a Lonely Path

A lone petal floats on the breeze,
Making friends with the laughing trees.
It twirls and spins, a solo act,
While the daisies play some fun impact.

It calls to the grass, 'Come join my game!'
But they stay rooted, all the same.
So off it goes with a little flair,
On a journey through the fragrant air.

It meets a twig who tells tall tales,
Of curious snails and wind-blown sails.
They share a chuckle under the sky,
Where petals alone can soar so high.

Though solitude wrapped it in a cloak,
This petal laughs at the jokes it spoke.
With nature's giggles keeping it warm,
It blooms in silence, free from harm.

The Cultivation of Calm

In a quiet patch where shadows loom,
The cucumbers plot to break the gloom.
They hold a meeting of grinning greens,
To master the art of serene scenes.

Zucchinis juggle while peas stand by,
Potatoes tell tales that make beans cry.
They sip on dew from morning's grace,
In laughter, they find their happy place.

They practice yoga, bending low,
While sunflowers bask in the gentlest glow.
With every shrug and rooty stretch,
They giggle so much, it's hard to catch.

In this calm, they grow bold and bright,
Each leaf a smile, a joyful sight.
In a chorus of plants, they softly sing,
In this stillness, they've found their spring.

In the Arms of the Moon

In the dark, the moonlight peeks,
Whispers secrets, the night softly speaks.
A cat in the corner, with shadows that dance,
Thinks it's a star, in a cosmic romance.

Chasing shadows, he trips on his tail,
Dreams of a world where he'd never fail.
Yet lonely he sits, with a sigh and a stretch,
Conceiving a plan, though none quite perfect.

From craters of cheese to a space-loving dog,
His imagination twirls like a misty fog.
With a grin, he ponders, then jumps to his feet,
A quest for companionship, isn't that sweet?

Then laughter erupts as he bumps into lore,
Finding a broomstick, he leaps to the floor.
In the arms of the moon, with the night as his muse,
It's the snippets of solitude that he'll always choose.

The Last Petal's Journey

A flower once bloomed in a pot by the gate,
Watched the world whirl, it was never too late.
With petals all pink, it was quite the sight,
But one gusty wind turned its day into night.

"Oh dear," said the flower, "I'm off with a swish,
To find out where petals go, what's their wish?"
It flew past a bird, who just shook its head,
"Why leave your safe home? You've a nice flower bed!"

Through gardens and pathways, it danced like a breeze,
Met dandelions knocking, "Come join us, please!"
They laughed until pollen filled up the air,
The last petal's journey led to comic despair.

In a puddle it landed, a splash and a sigh,
"I didn't mean to dive, just wanted to fly!"
So back to its pot, with a twist and a spin,
The flower learned solitude can also be fun.

The Heartbeat of Silence

In a room all alone, a sock begins to dance,
A lonely old shoe joins in for a chance.
With echoes of laughter from the corner they peek,
Inviting the dust bunnies, their friendship unique.

"Come join the fun!" the shoe gave a shout,
The sock rolled its eyes, "What's this all about?"
But soon they were waltzing, a twirl and a spin,
Creating a rhythm no one could pin.

The clock struck a pose, then ticked with a grin,
In the heartbeat of silence, let the party begin!
They stomped on the floor, to a beat of their own,
Finding joy in the stillness, in a world overgrown.

A lamp cheered them on, its light swayed with glee,
As they danced all night, wild and carefree.
In solitude's echo, laughter took flight,
For sometimes being alone brings the best kind of light.

A Lonely Horizon

On the edge of a cliff where the sky hugs the sea,
Stood a sentinel rock, feeling lonely and free.
It sighed at the clouds as they drifted on by,
Wishing for company, maybe a fish who could fly.

"Hey there, you seagull!" it called out with cheer,
But the bird just squawked, "I'm busy, my dear!"
The rock shook its head, "I'll just sit here and wait,
For conversations with waves, it's quite a nice fate."

The sun set ablaze, painting colors galore,
The rock felt quite pleased as it started to snore.
"Tomorrow," it mused with a wink and a grin,
"Maybe a dolphin will come to begin."

For in all of its solitude, humor would bloom,
With laughter and joy, even rocks find a room.
At the lonely horizon, where the sky meets the sea,
A quirky old rock found its wild destiny.

Beneath the Surface of Solitude

In a quiet room, the clock ticks loud,
Imagining a crowd, I laugh proud.
A sock puppet dances, says hello,
While I sip my drink, putting on a show.

Jellybeans chatter, what a delight,
They gossip about my socks every night.
With a banana peel slip, I take a dive,
Who knew lonely life could feel so alive?

The dust bunnies laugh as they collect,
All my secrets that I can't detect.
The cat on the shelf thinks it's a throne,
Remarking how I'm never alone.

Beneath my thoughts, a party resides,
With toast and tea, the fun abides.
In solitude's grip, they bring some cheer,
A hilarious chaos, I hold dear.

A Lonely Palette of Colors

Here's a canvas blank, lost in my mind,
No friend to share, I sit unrefined.
But wait, here comes purple with a bright grin,
It twirls and giggles, where do I begin?

Yellow joins in, wearing polka dots,
Declared it a party in forgotten spots.
They fling paint at me, oh what a sight,
Splattering joy from morning till night.

Green claims the corner, playing the lute,
While orange gets funky in a silly suit.
A weird little brush with a cantankerous heart,
Is making the masterpiece of my own art.

In the depths of this vibrant place,
Every stroke feels like a warm embrace.
A riot of shades, laughter in the air,
Who knew being alone could lead to such flair?

Fragments of a Dreaming Mind

In the abyss of thought, I softly drift,
With a sandwich on my head, I give a lift.
Dreams of dancing cheese in the moon's eye,
While juggling pineapples, I float high.

A fox in pajamas eats cereal with glee,
While I question why it's not just me.
The bed's a fairground, the sheets a slide,
Where giggles and nonsense often collide.

Each fragment's a riddle, a curious case,
With a turtle in a tuxedo pulling a race.
It zips past the clouds on a carrot-shaped bike,
Making laughter bloom like a tree on a hike.

Joy mingles here, in the wildest sights,
As I now discover the magic of nights.
In this dreamland, I'm never truly lone,
For every funny idea feels like home.

Solitary Reflections in a Pool

By the pond where the lilies wave, I stand,
A duck in a bowtie, oh isn't life grand?
It quacks about secrets that nobody knows,
While grass tickles toes, and giggles just flows.

I check my reflection, add a flower crown,
The frogs join the chorus, they never frown.
With a leap and a splash, they steal the scene,
While I sit and ponder, a king or a queen?

The water's a mirror, where I see the crew,
Dancing and laughing, inspiring the blues.
An old turtle winks, whispers wise lore,
"Embrace your own quirks, let your spirit soar!"

Alone at the pond, I find my delight,
With each silly moment, it feels just right.
In the laughter of water, I truly see,
Solitude's beauty can be joyous and free.

Unseen Gardens of the Mind

In the depths of my head, there's a party in bloom,
Dancing daisies with hats that fill up the room.
Forgetful tulips tell jokes that are keen,
While giggling weeds sip on soda and green.

A cactus in slippers does a little hula,
And puns from the pansies cause quite a tumult.
The roses decree that they're royalty here,
But droopy daffodils just cannot hold cheer.

Bumblebees buzz with a rhythm divine,
Tickling thoughts that dart here and there like fine wine.
In this garden of giggles, I start to unwind,
For laughter's the secret one seldom can find.

So I'll plant more dreams where the sun tends to play,
And dance with these blooms till they're withered away.
For inside my own mind, there's laughter each day,
In these unseen gardens, I'll happily stay.

Flowers of the Forgotten

In a corner of memory, blooms hide in a sway,
Waving to visitors who've lost their way.
With petal-thin laughter, they cackle and spin,
Telling tales of the past with a giggle and grin.

A buttercup whispers, 'Remember the time,
When we danced with the sunlight, all silver and rhyme?'
But the shadows just chuckle, 'We're stuck in our roots,
With no feet for the waltz, just these magical fruits.'

Forget-me-nots shout, 'We've plenty to say!'
But who's there to listen as they sway in dismay?
Each story's a laugh, sprinkled soft in the air,
And the daisies look hopeful, despite the despair.

So let's gather these blooms, make a crown of delight,
For laughter may echo on dark winter nights.
In flowers forgotten, let joy take its stand,
As we dance with our memories, hand-in-petaled-hand.

The Space Between Us

In a world of giggles, there's space for your toes,
And a worm who's a doctor with garden-like woes.
In every odd moment, we trip and we laugh,
As ants sport their briefcases and suit coats by half.

The breeze carries secrets of snickers and chimes,
While rocks play the sax with their melodic rhymes.
A daffy balloon floats, rehearsing its song,
In this quirky odd space, where all creatures belong.

Each thought is a dandelion, casting its seed,
A nostalgic dance where we both find the need.
To poke at the clouds and to giggle with glee,
In the area shared, just you, me, and thee.

So let's throw our worries to frogs and toadstools,
And sail through this laughter, it's nobody's rules.
With joy in the gaps that we fill with our jest,
In the spaces between us, our hearts feel the best.

A Solitary Sunbeam

A sunbeam awoke as the curtains were drawn,
Sipping on coffee, as bright as the dawn.
It stretched out its fingers, tickling the floor,
While shadows perform their faint opera once more.

"I'm here for a laugh!" the sunbeam declared,
But the dust bunnies giggled, quite blissfully ensnared.
They swirled and they twirled, in a chaotically bright,
Making friends with the cobwebs, a marvelous sight!

The wall clock just chuckled, "Time's on my side,"
While the lamp glowed with glee, taking it all in stride.
With each gentle moment, the sillies unite,
And the sunbeam feels merry in its whimsical flight.

So let's bask in this joy, let it linger and play,
As laughter falls cozy like sun's warm ballet.
For in this bright bubble, we'll be ever seen,
Where laughter's the sunshine, the glow in between.

The Tranquility of Empty Spaces

In quiet corners where dust bunnies play,
A tea party waits with a cat on display.
Cups of air fill with giggles and sighs,
As chairs have debates with the ceiling and skies.

My shadow dances, a partner so shy,
Whispers sweet nothings as it scoots by.
In this wide expanse of my charming abyss,
I toast with a biscuit: a one-person bliss.

The silence is loud, yet it tickles my face,
Like a prankster's tickle in empty space.
Birds sometimes chatter, but just out of view,
Scheming in silence, what mischief they'll do.

So here's to the void, with its quirks and its fun,
Where laughter erupts with nowhere to run.
It's a playground of whispers, of giggles and sighs,
In the pockets of time where the silly life lies.

Hidden Fauna of the Soul

In the jungle of thoughts where the odd critters roam,
A snail named Reginald claims it's his home.
He wears a top hat; so dapper, so neat,
Though his snazzy attire makes it hard to retreat.

The owls wear glasses, they're wise little folks,
Deciding if puns are delicious or jokes.
While turtles debate if they should wear shoes,
And flamingos ponder the latest cabooze.

In this secret abode, all thoughts come to play,
They stretch and they wiggle, they twirl and they sway.
An elephant chuckles, he's funny and free,
With a trunk full of giggles, oh wouldn't you see?

As breezes roll in, teasing leaves that will tease,
Creatures concoct antics with uttermost ease.
In the wilds of the mind where silliness grows,
They spiral and shimmer like glitter from prose.

Pollen of Thought

There's a buzz in the air that's as bright as a grin,
Thoughts float like bees, just waiting to spin.
With jars full of honey made sweet by the mind,
They dance through the flowers, leaving nothing behind.

Whimsical wishes flit, flutter, and dive,
Each idea a petal, feeling quite alive.
The laughter is sticky, the giggles like glue,
As bees trade their secrets with butterflies, too.

When the sun spills its rays all golden and round,
Silly thoughts scatter; they skip to the sound.
A waltz in the meadow where giggles collide,
The pollen of joy grows wild, far and wide.

So gather the laughter, let it dance in the breeze,
Join the buzzing chorus, do whatever you please.
In fields of delight, where the funny thoughts meet,
The heart finds a rhythm that's silly and sweet.

The Gentle Break of Dawn

In the arms of the morning, where silliness yawns,
Hiccups of light play peek-a-boo with the dawns.
Crickets are dozing; the sun grins awake,
Unruly and cheerful, it wobbles, a flake.

The toast pops up high, like a jester in flight,
With butter that wrestles for attention and light.
As the coffee does twirl, it spills tales to the cup,
While muffins keep secrets, they shush and sit up.

Birds tune their beaks to the morning's odd tune,
With melodies laughing at the sleepy cocoon.
The world bursts with giggles, as shadows retreat,
In this comedic ballet, all dancers repeat.

With every new dawn, the fun is reborn,
In the symphony silly, each heart is adorned.
So welcome the morning with chuckles and cheer,
Where laughter is woven, in daylight so clear.

Solitary Paths in the Woods

In the woods where no one goes,
My thoughts are silly, like a clown's nose.
Squirrels chatter, trees stand tall,
Yet it's my shadows that have a ball.

Twisting paths I walk alone,
Talking to rocks like they're my own.
Whispers of leaves make me chuckle,
As I trip over my own knuckle.

A bird sings offbeat, no real tune,
Dancing with branches, making me swoon.
If only the trees could crack a grin,
We'd laugh together, make mischief win.

Thus, I roam with misfits by my side,
A wacky crew in nature's wide slide.
In the woods, solitude's not a plight,
It's a quirky fiesta, pure delight!

Faint Echoes of Dawn

At dawn, the world is fast asleep,
I tiptoe around, avoiding the leap.
The coffee pot dances in my hand,
A real-life jester in my breakfast land.

Birds start chirping with a comedic tone,
Like they've had too much coffee of their own.
While I juggle toast and wobble too,
Maybe breakfast is a circus, who knew?

The sun peeks out with a yawning grin,
Awakening flowers, in a light spin.
I wave to the daisies, they bow back low,
In my solo show, they steal the show.

As day unfolds in awkward cheer,
I laugh at my socks, mismatched for a year.
Faint echoes of dawn bring chuckles bright,
In my private stage, everything's light!

Blossoms in a Quiet Corner

In the corner where shadows creep,
Petals giggle, secrets they keep.
A bumblebee wobbles, trips on a vine,
While I chuckle at nature's design.

Dandelions whisper in pastel hues,
Plotting pranks with the morning dew.
I join their gossip, a thorn in the lot,
Laughing at blossoms, the plotters they've got.

Sunshine spills on leaves with a cheer,
Like a comedian spreading joy near.
Every blossom, a jester of sort,
In my garden stage, nobody's caught.

So I sit and revel in this scene,
Where laughter blooms, bright and serene.
In a quiet corner, I find my view,
Surrounded by giggles, just me and my crew.

The Art of Being Alone

Embracing solitude like a cozy chair,
With mismatched cushions, I've no one to share.
I pour out my heart to an empty room,
Where the silence dances, in joy it will bloom.

A sock puppet joins for a late-night chat,
It shares the gossip, and we both laugh at that.
The cat has opinions on my fashion sense,
Dressed in pajamas, it's quite a pretense.

In my art of aloneness, I sketch bizarre jokes,
Painting life's colors with wacky strokes.
The clock ticks away, but who really cares?
Each tick-tock echo is a trumpet of flares.

So here's to the whimsy, the joy we can find,
In the quiet moments that dance in our mind.
The art of being alone is sweetly sincere,
With laughter and nonsense, I'm happy right here.

Buds Beneath the Surface

In a garden of giggles, they sprout,
With roots like noodles, they twist about.
Wiggling worms dance, with no care at all,
While petals of laughter grow ever tall.

Sunshine tickles leaves, a cheerful affair,
As chirping chipmunks quibble with flair.
Each bloom holds a secret, a joke or two,
In a world where the wild and the wacky are true.

Fostering the Forgotten

Forgotten friends beneath the dirt,
In their cozy darkness, they laugh and flirt.
Whispers of daisies make them all bright,
As they plan for the day, a comedic sight.

One sprout tells a joke that's terribly lame,
Yet somehow, all chuckle, they're all to blame.
In the quiet corners, the laughter rings,
Like a secret society of silly things.

Fragments of Peace

Amidst the stillness, a tickle of cheer,
Tiny buds giggle, 'We're glad you're here!'
A chipper chortle from under the ground,
Echoes of joy in the peace they've found.

A sunflower winks with a pollen-filled grin,
While the daisies debate where to begin.
In patches of laughter, where quiet meets fun,
They savor the calm, one pun at a run.

Emergence of the Unaccompanied

With solo ambitions, they stretch and yawn,
Each bud a rebel, from dusk until dawn.
Who needs companions when you can gymnastic?
A flower's solo act, hilariously fantastic!

Bouncing alone, quite the humor parade,
With ruffled-haired blooms, they won't be dismayed.
In the realm of the lonely, fun reigns supreme,
Where dreams of grandeur reflect in each beam.

Solitary Blooms

In a garden where no critters dare,
A sunflower whispers, "Is anyone there?"
The daisies giggle, a strange little crew,
With no one to judge, they dance like they do.

A lone little frog, with a crown made of weeds,
Croaks a song to the plants, as if they have needs.
The tulips chuckle, in colors so bright,
While petals burst forth in a whimsical delight.

The wind blows a tickle, a breezy slapstick,
A spin on the stem gives a quirky little kick.
They revel in solitude, they're free as can be,
Throwing petals in laughter, all wild and carefree.

So here's to the oddballs, alone yet alive,
In their own funny world, they laugh and they thrive.
With no worries of crowds, they invent little games,
In the silence they flourish, with joy that inflames.

Beneath the Silent Sky

Under a vast dome where nobody stirs,
A cloud takes a nap, while a bird softly purrs.
The sun grins wide, with no one to frown,
On a horizon where giggles are the crown.

A cactus stands straight, with a quip on its spine,
"I'm prickly but lovely, it's just how I shine!"
The stars come out, throwing winks from above,
Twinkling in silence, like whispers of love.

The moon checks its watch, and rolls its bright eyes,
"To be loyal to night, it's a laugh in disguise."
With shadows that dance in a comical fight,
They glide through the darkness, all merry and light.

So let's raise a toast to the cosmic parade,
Where laughter is born and silly plans are made.
In the hush of the night, where dreams take a climb,
There's humor in solitude, like a silly old rhyme.

Roots of Reflection

In a forest where whispers tickle the trees,
A squirrel looks serious, "Now where's my keys?"
The ferns roll their eyes and the oaks just shrug,
While a hedgehog throws shade, feeling snug as a bug.

A tangle of roots share stories so odd,
"A fork in the path? Oh, give me a nod!"
They're busting with laughter at who's taking a stand,
"Just follow your heart, or the oddest of strands."

The mushrooms debate who's the king of the soil,
A witty little toad calls it all just a foil.
"Let's have a grand picnic, with snacks from the ground,
In this quiet, we find the best joy to be found."

So here's to the roots, with their jokes and their schemes,
In the silence of nature, they flourish in dreams.
Solitude's magic, a whimsical friend,
With laughter and joy that will never end.

A Meadow of Forgotten Dreams

In a quiet old meadow, where daisies now lie,
A forgetful old bee flits, "Where's the next pie?"
The butterflies giggle, catching rays in their wings,
While sunlight sings softly of whimsical things.

The grass has its secrets, all wild and untamed,
"Remember that time we all played a game?"
A rabbit pops up, with a wink and a shiver,
"Let's dance like no one's watching, we're blissfully clever!"

A breeze brings a chuckle, tickling the blooms,
"Does anyone know where the wild laughter zooms?"
Each petal's a story, each stem shows a grin,
Where solitude's laughter dances within.

So let's prance through the meadow, in this world like a dream,
Where a giggle can spiral into life's sweetest theme.
In the tapestry woven with joy so supreme,
There's funny in lonely, or so it would seem.

The Rhythm of Being Alone

In my room, I dance alone,
Two left feet, but I've grown.
The cat watches with a glare,
While I twirl without a care.

Kitchen beats are my new song,
Burning toast? Can't be wrong!
Singing loud to silent walls,
Echoes laugh as silence calls.

Sock puppets join my play,
On this sunlit, quirky day.
Mismatched patterns full of cheer,
Who knew alone could feel so near?

When the fridge hums a tune,
I groove beneath the silver moon.
In my bubble, joy prevails,
Found my groove in solo trails.

A Tapestry of Solitude

I sit and knit my wishes tight,
With yarn that glows, oh what a sight!
Purls of laughter, stitches of cheer,
My imaginary friends all near.

The tea pot whistles, sings along,
A jazzy tune, a perfect song.
As tea leaves swirl, I debate,
If solitude can truly be great?

Spinning tales with every thread,
A scarf for me, a hat instead.
It's tough to wear a knitted frown,
When every stitch is a silly clown.

As I unravel all my thoughts,
My pet rock shares the dreams I've sought.
We giggle softly at the scene,
In this quiet space, I reign supreme.

The Untold Story of a Flower

Once a seed in a pot so round,
Dreamed of colors, glories found.
But the sun just seemed to tease,
Sunbathing, feeling quite at ease.

A daisy tried to shake its roots,
While evergreens wore sturdy boots.
Petals shared some wild gossip jest,
As the soil whispered, 'Take your rest.'

Along came rain, with quite a splash,
Drowned the dreams—now here's the clash!
"Stop moaning! Bloom, you silly sprout!"
Laughter echoed, whimsy about.

At last, it bloomed, a vibrant hue,
Told its tale, a joy to view.
Turns out silence's not so bad,
When solitude births the least sad.

Whispers Among the Roots

Beneath the ground where shadows creep,
The roots gossip and secrets keep.
"I heard the daffodils had fun,"
Said one old root, "Oh, how they run!"

While worms wiggle, plotting schemes,
Unraveled laughter cloaked in dreams.
A dandelion, wise and bold,
Jokes about adventures untold.

"Let's throw a party down below,
Bring the beetles, they'll steal the show!"
The mushrooms chuckled, "Count us in!"
With cheeky grins, they spin and spin.

So amidst the quiet, life unfolds,
In whispers shared, sweet stories told.
Who knew the dirt could sprout such cheer?
Solitude sings when friends are near.

www.ingramcontent.com/pod-product-compliance
Lightning Source LLC
Chambersburg PA
CBHW070314120526
44590CB00017B/2678